THE CIVIL WAR

Union soldiers rush to beat back a Confederate attack
in one of the ten thousand battles that made the Civil War
the bloodiest conflict in American history.

AMERICAN TRAGEDY
THE
CIVIL
WAR

BY ALDEN R. CARTER

FRANKLIN WATTS

New York ★ Chicago ★ London ★ Toronto ★ Sydney
A First Book

ACKNOWLEDGMENTS

Many thanks to all who helped with *The Civil War,*
particularly my editor, Reni Roxas; my mother,
Hilda Carter Fletcher; and my friends Barbara Feinberg
and Dean Markwardt. As always, my wife, Carol,
deserves much of the credit.

Maps by William J. Clipson

Cover photography copyright © Time-Life Books Inc., 1985/Larry Sherer

Photographs copyright © : Private Collection, Houston, TX: p. 2; The
Metropolitan Museum of Art, Gift of Mr. & Mrs. Carl Stoekel, 1897, (97.5)
p. 13; New York Public Library, Picture Collection: pp. 14, 16 bottom, 23,
25 bottom, 31, 34, 37, 45 top, 49 top, 51; The White House Historical
Association, photograph by The National Geographic Society: p. 16 top;
Historical Pictures Service, Chicago: pp. 19, 20, 25 top, 32, 38 top, 49
bottom, 50, 55; Brown Brothers, Sterling, PA: p. 28; Time-Life Books Inc.,
1985/Larry Sherer: pp. 36, 38 bottom; Library of Congress: p. 45 bottom;
The Lincoln Museum, Fort Wayne, IN: p. 54.

Library of Congress Cataloging-in-Publication Data

Carter, Alden R.
The Civil War / by Alden R. Carter
p.   cm. — (A First book)
Includes bibliographical references and index.
Summary: Examines the war that cost more than 500,000 lives, from
the Battle of First Bull Run to the final surrender of the Confederate Army in 1865.
ISBN 0-531-20039-6 (lib. bdg.) / ISBN 0-531-15653-2 (pbk.)
1. United States—History—Civil War, 1861-1865—Juvenile
literature. [1. United States—History—Civil War, 1861-1865.]
I. Title.   II. Series.
E468.C25 1992
973.7—dc20   91-14752 CIP AC

CONTENTS

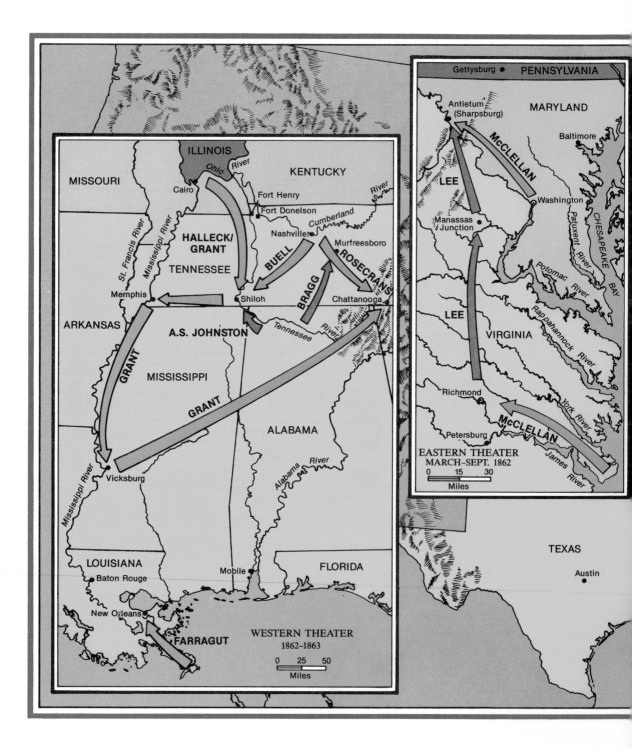

ILLINOIS

MISSOURI

KENTUCKY

Ohio River

Cairo

Fort Henry
Fort Donelson

Cumberland River

Nashville

HALLECK/
GRANT

TENNESSEE

St. Francis River

Mississippi River

BUELL

Murfreesboro

ROSECRANS

Memphis

Shiloh

BRAGG

Chattanooga

ARKANSAS

A.S. JOHNSTON

Tennessee River

GRANT

MISSISSIPPI

GRANT

ALABAMA

Alabama River

Vicksburg

Mississippi River

LOUISIANA

Baton Rouge

Mobile

FLORIDA

New Orleans

FARRAGUT

WESTERN THEATER
1862-1863

0   25   50
Miles

Gettysburg   PENNSYLVANIA

Antietam
(Sharpsburg)

MARYLAND

Baltimore

McCLELLAN

LEE

Manassas
Junction

Washington

Patuxent River

CHESAPEAKE BAY

Potomac River

LEE

Rappahannock River

VIRGINIA

Richmond

Petersburg

McCLELLAN

York River

James River

EASTERN THEATER
MARCH-SEPT. 1862

0   15   30
Miles

TEXAS

Austin

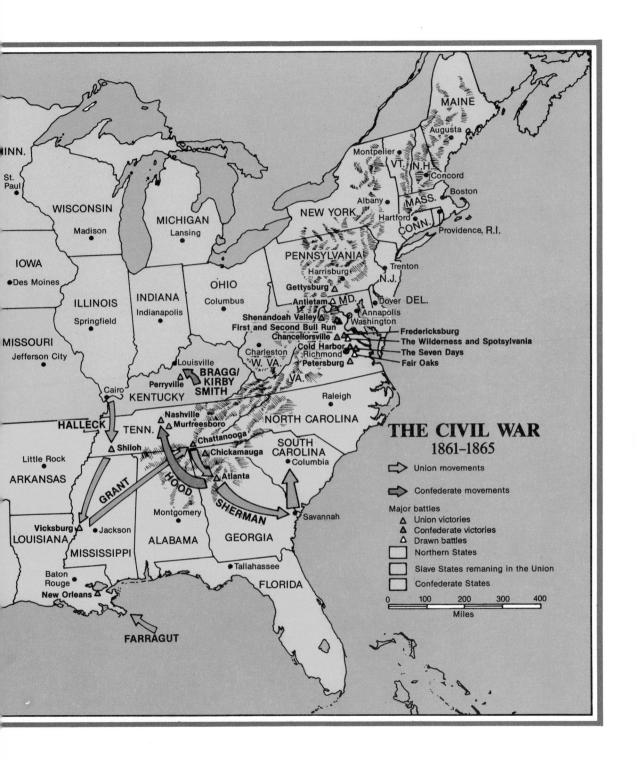

MAINE

Augusta

Montpelier

VT. N.H.

Concord

NEW YORK

Albany

MASS.

Boston

Hartford

CONN.

Providence, R.I.

St. Paul

MINN.

WISCONSIN

MICHIGAN

Madison

Lansing

PENNSYLVANIA

Harrisburg

Trenton

N.J.

IOWA

Des Moines

ILLINOIS

INDIANA

OHIO

Columbus

Gettysburg △

Dover DEL.

Antietam △ MD.

Annapolis

Shenandoah Valley △

Washington

First and Second Bull Run △

Fredericksburg

Springfield

Indianapolis

Chancellorsville △

The Wilderness and Spotsylvania

MISSOURI

Charleston

Cold Harbor

The Seven Days

Jefferson City

W. VA.

Richmond

Fair Oaks

Louisville

Petersburg △

Cairo

Perryville

BRAGG/

KIRBY

SMITH

VA.

KENTUCKY

Raleigh

HALLECK

TENN.

Nashville △

NORTH CAROLINA

Little Rock

△ Shiloh

Murfreesboro △

Chattanooga △

Chickamauga △

SOUTH

CAROLINA

THE CIVIL WAR

1861–1865

ARKANSAS

GRANT

HOOD

Columbia ●

Atlanta △

⇨ Union movements

Montgomery

SHERMAN

Savannah

⇨ Confederate movements

Vicksburg △

● Jackson

Major battles

LOUISIANA

△ Union victories

MISSISSIPPI

ALABAMA

GEORGIA

△ Confederate victories

△ Drawn battles

Baton

Rouge

● Tallahassee

Northern States

New Orleans △

FLORIDA

Slave States remaning in the Union

Confederate States

0   100   200   300   400

Miles

FARRAGUT

FOR A MASTER WRITER,
JIM FLETCHER

ONE

THE HOUSE DIVIDED

★

WITH BANDS playing and crowds cheering, two American armies marched off to war in the spring of 1861. Hardly anyone in the Union army of the North or the Confederate army of the South expected a long war. Dreams of quick victory and easy glory filled the heads of the young soldiers. Few guessed that four years of misery, blood, and horror lay ahead.

The American Civil War cost more lives than all the other wars in United States history *combined*. Fully one of every four soldiers who enlisted in the struggle died of wounds or disease. Out of this terrible suffering came a stronger and more united nation. Yet some of the scars of America's greatest war remain even today.

The Civil War had no single cause. North and South had never been comfortable partners in the Union of the states and had grown steadily apart in the first half of the 1800s.

European visitors often commented that the two regions were so unlike in attitudes, cultures, and economies that they seemed like different countries. The plantation system dominated the Southern way of life. On large farms, black slaves cultivated crops of tobacco, rice, and—most important of all—cotton. While most Southern merchants, tradesmen, and small farmers owned few or no slaves, they supported the system and accepted the leadership of the rich and well-educated plantation owners.

The North did not have the South's rigid class system, with a wealthy few at the top and a great number of slaves at the bottom. The North's economy was based on small farms and a growing number of factories. The North seemed a busier place, as floods of immigrants swelled its cities. Neither needing slaves nor believing in the morality of owning human beings, most Northern states outlawed slavery.

The rapid growth of the North worried Southerners. Most Southerners believed in a loose Union of largely independent states, while most Northerners favored a close Union under a strong national government. Congress argued this and the other issues dividing the two regions. More voters gave the North more seats in the House of Representatives. However, with two seats for each state, the Senate was almost equally divided, giving Southern senators the power to block legislation threatening to Southern interests. With Congress often deadlocked, a series of weak presidents and a Southern majority on the Supreme Court did little to resolve the differences between the two regions.

The settlement of the West threatened the balance between North and South. As the nation expanded westward toward the Pacific Ocean, Southern settlers demanded the right to take slavery into the territories that would one day become states. Northerners, particularly abolitionists (those who wanted to "abolish" slavery), fought any spread of slavery. On several occasions, the issue almost resulted in war between North and South before Congress could work out agreements to save the Union for a while longer. These compromises divided the western territories into slave and free states. The admission of one free state for one slave state preserved the equal power of North and South in the Senate.

However, none of the compromises could work forever, and the slavery issue continued to pull the nation apart. In the 1850s, the nation's two major political parties, the Democrats and the Whigs, split into Northern and Southern wings. Most Northern Whigs soon joined the new Republican party, which firmly opposed slavery, while Southern Whigs joined Southern Democrats in fighting any controls on slavery. Northern Democrats, led by Senator Stephen A. Douglas of Illinois, worked out another compromise. The Kansas-Nebraska Act of 1854 allowed each territory to decide for itself whether to enter the Union as a slave or free state. The compromise was a failure. Instead of insuring peace, it touched off bloody fighting in Kansas as proslavery and antislavery settlers tried to grab control of the voting.

While North and South argued over "Bleeding Kansas," the Supreme Court made a tense situation worse. The Court ruled in the complicated *Dred Scott* decision of 1857 that Congress could not ban slavery in the territories. The decision called into question the legality of outlawing slavery anywhere, even in states that had long been "free." Uproar swept the country. In the middle of the deepening crisis, a little-known Illinois lawyer and former congressman met Senator Douglas to debate the slavery issue in the Illinois senatorial campaign of 1858. Although Abraham Lincoln lost the election, his powerful speeches won him national fame. In one speech he declared, "a house divided against itself cannot stand." Events soon proved him right.

In October 1859, a wild abolitionist named John Brown and a small band of followers captured the army post at Harpers Ferry, Virginia. Brown planned to arm thousands of slaves with the weapons stored in the arsenal. Brown was quickly captured, tried, and hung for treason. To Southerners, who had long feared a slave revolt, Brown was a monster. Many in the North saw him as a hero who died bravely for his beliefs.

As the nation threatened to break apart, Congress deadlocked in stormy debate. Some members even carried pis-

The abolitionist warrior John Brown (1800–1859)
pauses on his way to the gallows to kiss a black child.

tols in case argument turned into actual fighting. President James Buchanan, an honest but weak leader, longed for an end to his term of office. In a bitter four-way race, Abraham Lincoln led the Republicans to a narrow victory in the presidential election of 1860. Although Lincoln promised not

Newspapers spread vicious political propaganda during the Civil War. In this 1861 political cartoon, an enraged American eagle tears apart the traitorous offspring in its nest of states.

to interfere with slavery where it already existed, seven Southern states took his election as a signal to declare their independence. South Carolina, Mississippi, Florida, Alabama, Georgia, Louisiana, and Texas seceded from the Union to form a new nation, the Confederate States of America, or the Confederacy.

Southerners argued that since each state had joined the Union voluntarily, each had a right to leave it at any time. Lincoln and a majority of Northerners disagreed, arguing that the Union was permanent and that states could not secede simply because they disagreed with the results of an election. The secession argument swept the question of slavery aside for the moment. Patriots North and South believed that they were defending the ideals of self-government. Southerners accused "Yankees" of trying to destroy their way of life, leaving them no choice but to secede from the Union. Northerners saw the South's secession as an attack on America's "glorious experiment in democracy." If the South succeeded in breaking the Union, the world would never again believe that a free people could govern themselves.

Lincoln was sworn in as president on March 4, 1861. He delivered a carefully worded speech, standing firm against secession but offering friendship to the rebel states if they returned to the Union. His words were particularly aimed at the eight slave states that had yet to choose between the Confederacy and the Union.

Left: Called "a bumpkin, a gorilla, and a buffoon" by prominent members of his own party, President Abraham Lincoln would prove to be a leader of astonishing strength.

Below: Confederate troops open fire on the federal garrison of Fort Sumter on April 12, 1861.

For a month America hung on the edge of war with neither side wanting the blame for firing the first shot. President Jefferson Davis of the Confederacy demanded the surrender of Fort Sumter, located in the harbor of Charleston, South Carolina. Lincoln refused, but promised to send only food to the fort as long as a chance for peace remained. Worried that the Confederacy would crumble if the stalemate continued, Davis sent orders to General Pierre Beauregard at Charleston. Early on the morning of April 12, 1861, Beauregard's Confederate cannons opened fire on Fort Sumter. Outnumbered and outgunned, the fort's soldiers surrendered thirty-three hours later.

News of the fall of Fort Sumter brought wild rejoicing in the South and terrible anger in the North. Virginia, North Carolina, Tennessee, and Arkansas joined the Confederacy. Delaware declared for the Union, as did northwestern Virginia, which became the state of West Virginia in 1863. Union troops occupied Maryland before it could vote, and a small Union army in Missouri quickly won the fight for that state. Kentucky announced that it would sit out the war, but a Southern invasion late in the year so angered Kentuckians that they declared for the Union.

War fever gripped the land. Rivers of men rushed to join the armies of North and South. As the world watched, brother prepared to fight brother, neighbor to strike neighbor, and American to slaughter American.

TWO

END OF
EASY DREAMS

★

ON JULY 21, 1861, the two armies that dreamed of quick and easy victory met near the railroad junction of Manassas, Virginia, less than 30 miles (50 km) south of Washington, D.C. Civilian spectators from the nation's capital spread blankets and opened picnic baskets as the Union army of General Irvin McDowell attacked across a small stream called Bull Run.

The smoke of cannon and rifle fire soon hid the fighting, but reports came that the Union troops had broken the Confederate line and were driving the Southerners from the battlefield. By the end of the afternoon, the war would be over and the Union saved. Then the Union attack stumbled. On Henry House Hill, a Confederate brigade under General Thomas J. Jackson held its position. An officer trying to rally his fleeing men pointed to Jackson: "Look, there stands Jackson like a stone wall!" The retreating soldiers re-formed

their line and held off attack after attack by the Union troops. Tired and disorganized, the Union soldiers began falling back. A sudden counterattack by fresh Confederate troops threw the Northerners into a panic. They started running up the road toward Washington. The spectators dropped their picnic baskets and fled with them.

It rained all that night, as thousands of discouraged Union

On July 21, 1861, the Confederates routed Union troops at the Battle of Bull Run (Manassas) between Washington and the Confederate capital of Richmond, Virginia.

After the disaster at Bull Run, Lincoln appointed General
George McClellan to command the Union Army of the Potomac.

soldiers streamed into Washington. In the gray dawn, President Lincoln half expected to see the victorious Confederate army marching up Pennsylvania Avenue toward the White House. Yet victory had left the Confederate army nearly as battered and disorganized as the Union army. After a few tense days, fresh Union troops arrived from the north to guard Washington.

Lincoln replaced the luckless McDowell with a dashing young general, George B. McClellan. Only thirty-two, "Little Mac" was a brilliant organizer. He set about making soldiers of the raw recruits who had fought at the Battle of Bull Run, or Manassas as it was called in the South. By the fall of 1861, the Union Army of the Potomac was the best-drilled, best-fed, and best-equipped army in America — perhaps in the world. But could it fight? The president urged McClellan to advance on the Confederate capital of Richmond, Virginia, before winter weather turned the roads to mud. The general stalled, insisting that he needed more time and more soldiers. Fall turned to winter with the Army of the Potomac still encamped outside Washington.

Only 100 miles (160 km) away in Richmond, President Jefferson Davis also had problems. The handsome former senator knew that the Confederacy faced long odds in its fight for independence. The South had nine million people — less than half the population of the North. Four million were black slaves, leaving a white population of only five million to provide soldiers for the army. The North had twice as many miles of railroad as the South to move armies and supplies. Northern factories produced five times more goods than Southern factories. The Confederacy would have to buy almost all its weapons in Europe with money earned by selling its cotton crop. But the Union navy was already blocking the South's trade with Europe, and the Confederacy had almost no navy to defend its long coast. Davis knew that the South's best hope lay in persuading Great Britain and France to send their mighty navies to end the Union blockade. However, to win their help, Confederate armies would have to win victories on the battlefield.

Fortunately for Davis, the Confederacy had advantages too. It did not have to invade the North, only defend its home soil. Most Southern soldiers had experience with horses, rifles, and outdoor living. The South's armies were led by experienced officers who had resigned from the United States Army rather than fight against their native states. (Davis himself was a former army officer and secretary of war.) In the North, many people were against the war. After one or two smashing Southern victories, Northerners might raise such a howl that Lincoln would have to agree to peace.

Everyone waited for the next test of strength. It came in the West. Davis had given General Albert Sidney Johnston the nearly impossible job of defending the Confederacy from the Appalachian Mountains to the western border of Arkansas. Through the heart of this vast area flowed the broad Mississippi River, the natural pathway for a Union effort to cut the Confederacy in two. Union General Henry Halleck meant to take the Mississippi from Johnston. At his headquarters in St. Louis, Missouri, "Old Brains" Halleck studied his maps. Confederate cannons on the high bluff at Columbus, Kentucky, blocked the way south. Halleck decided to bypass this obstacle by sending an army up the Tennessee and Cumberland rivers in a long sweep that would bring it back to the Mississippi at Memphis, Tennessee, far below Columbus.

Facing a huge disadvantage in population and industrial might,
the South depended on its soldiers' bravery, the skill of its
generals, and the iron determination of President Jefferson Davis.

To carry out his plan, Halleck chose Brigadier General
Ulysses S. Grant. It was a choice that would change the course
of the war. At forty, Grant had hardly been a success in life.
A graduate of the United States Military Academy at West
Point, he had served ably in the Mexican War (1846–48),
but drinking and gambling had led to his resignation from
the army. As a civilian, he had failed as a farmer and a busi-
nessman before returning to the army after the Battle of
Fort Sumter.

War brought out talents long hidden in Grant. He cared nothing for parades and fancy uniforms. He had a job to do, and he went about it in a quiet, steady manner. He took his army up the Tennessee River on transports. The Union navy's gunboats forced the surrender of Fort Henry, and Grant marched his men across the narrow strip of land to Fort Donelson on the Cumberland River. After a sharp battle, the fort's commander asked for terms of surrender with the hope that Grant would allow the Confederates to go home on the promise not to fight again. Grant answered: "unconditional surrender." On February 16, 1862, 12,000 Confederate soldiers laid down their rifles, and the North had a new hero in "Unconditional Surrender" Grant.

Grant led his army south to attack the vital railroad junction at Corinth, Mississippi. Meanwhile, another Union army under General Don Carlos Buell advanced against General Johnston's Confederates in central Kentucky. Johnston was in a fix. If Grant took Corinth, the Confederacy would lose its major east-west railroad line, Memphis would fall, and the Union would control another long stretch of the Mississippi. Somehow Johnston had to stop Grant. He pulled out of Kentucky and central Tennessee ahead of Buell's advance.

Grant's army was at Pittsburg Landing, only 20 miles (32 km) from the railroad junction, by the time Johnston gathered his scattered forces at Corinth. At dawn on April 6, Johnston's army smashed into Grant's camp. The Battle

Above: Artists often invented romantic battle scenes, as in this painting,
The Charge of General Grant at Shiloh. In reality, Grant was too busy
to risk either his time or his life in a charge during the two-day slugfest.
Below: Lugging their primitive, bulky equipment from battlefield to battlefield,
Civil War photographers brought home images of the true cost of war.

of Shiloh became a huge, confused fight as eighty thousand inexperienced soldiers slugged it out on a narrow, rocky plain around the Shiloh church. The Confederate attack forced the Union troops back toward the Tennessee River. A Union division in the center held along a road bank running through a grove of trees. A dozen times the Confederates charged the "Hornet's Nest," only to be thrown back with heavy losses. Johnston himself led the final charge. A bullet tore into his leg, and he bled to death as the Union troops in the Hornet's Nest finally surrendered.

The desperate courage of the Union soldiers in the Hornet's Nest gave the rest of the army time to form a new line. Steadied by Grant, the Union troops held their ground with their backs to the river until dark. During the night, fresh troops crossed from the far shore of the Tennessee. The next morning Grant's army came roaring back to retake all the ground lost the day before. At nightfall, the Southerners began withdrawing toward Corinth.

North and South were stunned by the losses at Shiloh. The battle cost 23,741 dead, wounded, or captured soldiers. In two days, the armies had suffered more losses than all American armies in all the nation's previous wars. An observer later stated that a man could have walked the 2 miles (3.2 km) across the battlefield on the bodies of dead soldiers without touching the ground.

After Shiloh no one believed in easy victories.

THREE

EDGE OF
DISASTER

★

EVERYWHERE he looked in the spring of 1862, Confederate President Jefferson Davis saw approaching disaster. In the West, Halleck and Grant's large Union army was forcing the Confederates from Corinth, while Union gunboats took Memphis. In the East, McClellan's mighty Army of the Potomac readied for a drive on the Confederate capital of Richmond. Along the coast, the Union navy grabbed Southern offshore islands and coastal forts as it tightened its blockade.

A month before the Battle of Shiloh, the Confederacy had sent its secret weapon to break the naval blockade of Norfolk, Virginia. Built on the hull of the former Federal frigate *Merrimack,* the ironclad ship *Virginia* looked like a floating shed. Although ugly, slow, and clumsy, it was a fearsome weapon. Its iron-plated housing protected ten big guns, and its iron nose could smash through the hull of any wooden ship in the blockading fleet.

On March 8, the *Virginia* surprised and destroyed two Union ships and drove a third aground. The Confederates were overjoyed; it seemed that nothing could stop the *Virginia*. But the next morning a strange-looking Union ship steamed to meet the *Virginia*. One watcher described the Union ironclad *Monitor* as looking like "a cheesebox on a raft." The cheesebox was actually a swiveling turret housing two huge guns.

The *Monitor* and the *Virginia* battered each other for four hours in history's first battle between ironclad ships. The fight ended in a draw as the two ships turned away to repair damage. They never fought again. Unable to get past the *Monitor,* the *Virginia* lay bottled up in port until sunk by its crew two months later to prevent capture by a Union army. Both sides rushed to build more ironclads, but Union shipyards turned out more and better ships. Union *Monitor*s would tighten the blockade and help win control of the inland rivers.

In history's first fight between armored warships, the Confederate ironclad *Virginia* and the Union ironclad *Monitor* battered each other in the four-hour Battle of Hampton Roads on March 9, 1862. Inset: The volunteer crew of the *Monitor* poses on deck.

President Davis soon had more bad news to add to his worries. A powerful Union fleet under Captain David Farragut threatened New Orleans, Louisiana, the South's largest and most important city. Ninety miles (145 km) below the city, two forts guarded the mouth of the Mississippi. The Confederate gunners were confident that they could blow apart any Union warship foolish enough to head upstream. Farragut took the chance. Early on the morning of April 24, his thirteen wooden ships made a dash for New Orleans. Cannon fire from the forts lit the broad river, but ten of the Union ships made it past. They shot apart a small fleet of Confederate gunboats and steamed north toward New Orleans. The great city surrendered the next day.

Many people in both North and South thought Richmond would be next. General McClellan's Army of the Potomac had landed on the Yorktown Peninsula near Norfolk and was preparing to march on the Confederate capital with over 100,000 men. Davis called on General Robert E. Lee to save Richmond. He could not have chosen better.

At fifty-five, the handsome, gray-bearded Lee had been a soldier for more than thirty years. When the Civil War began, President Lincoln had offered him command of the Union army. Lee, however, could not bring himself to fight against his native Virginia. He declined and rode south to offer his services to the Confederacy. After a year of minor assignments, he now had a job worthy of his talents.

Lee moved quickly, gathering scattered Confederate

forces and strengthening Richmond's defenses. General McClellan proved his best ally. Little Mac had trained a great army, but he was unwilling to risk it. It took the Army of the Potomac two full months to advance the 60 miles (100 km) up the peninsula to the outskirts of Richmond. By then, Lee had gathered 60,000 men under General Joseph Johnston. On May 31, 1862, Johnston attacked McClellan

On April 24, 1862, the Union fleet of Captain David Farragut ran past the blazing guns of the Confederate forts guarding the Mississippi River below New Orleans.

Gray-bearded General Robert E. Lee engineered the
greatest Confederate victories of the war. To his right
is the brilliant General Thomas J. "Stonewall" Jackson;
standing is General P. G. T. Beauregard.

at the Battle of Fair Oaks (called Seven Pines in the South).
A day of hard fighting brought the Union advance to a stand-
still. Johnston was wounded, and Lee took over command
of the army in the field.

McClellan called on Washington for more troops, but
Lincoln had already sent every available man to chase "Stonewall" Jackson's Confederate army in the Shenandoah Valley.
Since the end of March, Jackson had been defeating one
small Union army after another in a brilliant campaign still
studied in military colleges. He now dodged the fresh army

sent by Lincoln and hurried south to join Lee at Richmond. On June 26, Lee attacked McClellan, opening a daring series of battles called the Seven Days. A week and five battles later, McClellan and his bloodied army were in retreat. The South had found its great general.

McClellan's failure caused an uproar in the North. More and more people demanded peace at any price. Under attack from all sides, Lincoln looked for ways to revive the Union cause. It was time to face the issue of slavery. Lincoln decided to issue a presidential order freeing slaves in the "states in rebellion." He hoped that the Emancipation Proclamation would give the North a new sense of purpose, encourage thousands of slaves to escape to Union lines, and discourage European countries from siding with the South.

In July Lincoln read his proclamation to two of his advisers. They worried that it would seem like a sign of weakness to make the proclamation public after Union defeats. Lincoln agreed to wait until the North won a victory. Meanwhile, he brought General Halleck to Washington to straighten out the administration of all the Union armies.

Robert E. Lee did not intend to wait for victories but to win them. While McClellan withdrew his army from the Yorktown Peninsula to Washington, Lee captured the Union supply base at Manassas Junction — the site a year earlier of the first major battle of the war. A Union army under General John Pope attacked but was thoroughly whipped and driven back to Washington. Lee marched into Maryland,

Lincoln's cabinet approved the Emancipation Proclamation
but worried that it would seem a desperate gesture in a season
of defeat. Lincoln agreed to wait for a Union victory.

carrying the war into the North for the first time. He knew that Washington was too strongly defended to attack, but the capture of Philadelphia or Baltimore might bring recognition of Southern independence by Britain and France and force Lincoln to end the war.

Lee's first target was the Union arsenal at Harpers Ferry and its 12,000 men. He issued orders to his generals, but someone carelessly dropped a copy. It was found by Union soldiers several days later. An alert officer sent it to McClellan. Boasting that he at last had the means to crush "Bobby" Lee, Little Mac pushed his army forward—but slowly. On September 17, 1862, the two great armies met along Antietam Creek near Sharpsburg, Maryland.

The Battle of Antietam produced the bloodiest day of the war. With 87,000 men to Lee's 41,000, McClellan should have won a great victory. Instead, he badly mismanaged his army, never ordering an attack all along the line and failing to get a third of his army into action. Lee coolly shifted troops to threatened points as reinforcements rushed to the battlefield. They arrived in late afternoon, just in time to block a final Union attack.

Everyone expected the battle to continue the next day, but McClellan did nothing, and Lee's army withdrew across the Potomac River into Virginia. It had been a victory of sorts for the Union, and Lincoln decided to issue the Emancipation Proclamation on September 22, 1862. The proclamation

In the single bloodiest day of the Civil War, the Union army turned back
the Confederate invasion of Maryland at the Battle of Antietam
(near Sharpsburg) on September 17, 1862. It was the victory
Lincoln needed before issuing the Emancipation Proclamation.

promised freedom only for slaves inside the Confederacy,
not in areas that had remained loyal to the Union or were
held by Northern armies, but it was a giant first step in lift-
ing a great injustice from the backs of millions of black
people. Soon tens of thousands of former slaves were work-
ing for the Union armies as teamsters and laborers. By the
war's end, more than 100,000 blacks would serve the Union
cause as soldiers.

Lincoln was fed up with McClellan. Too many times

Escorted by President Lincoln and
General McClellan, Liberty rides triumphantly
aboard the chariot of Emancipation.

Above: Frustrated with General McClellan's inaction, Lincoln replaced him with General Ambrose Burnside in November 1862. But Burnside bumbled, suffering a terrible defeat at Fredericksburg, Virginia, on December 13, 1862.

Left: Still looking for a general to match Robert E. Lee, Lincoln appointed General Joseph "Fighting Joe" Hooker. But the brilliant Lee thrashed Hooker at the Battle of Chancellorsville, Virginia, on May 1–4, 1863.

Little Mac had failed to move quickly or to use the full power of his army. In November, Lincoln replaced McClellan with General Ambrose Burnside, ordering him to destroy Lee's army and take Richmond. On the far side of the Rappahannock River, Lee and his Army of Northern Virginia waited to see if this new Union general would fight. He did, but poorly. On December 13, the Army of the Potomac crossed the river and charged up the bluffs at Fredericksburg, Virginia. Lee's men shot them down by the thousands. The Army of the Potomac retreated once again to heal its wounds. Lincoln fired Burnside, replacing him with General Joseph "Fighting Joe" Hooker.

In late April 1863, Hooker ordered the Army of the Potomac across the Rappahannock west of Fredericksburg. Lee's army was waiting. The Battle of Chancellorsville (May 1–4, 1863) showed Lee at his most brilliant. Outnumbered by more than two to one, Lee broke all the rules in the military textbooks. He divided his army, sending Stonewall Jackson to make a lightning attack on the far end of Hooker's line. Lee's slashing attacks completely unnerved Hooker. As usual, Union soldiers paid in blood and pride for their general's bumbling. By dawn on May 5, they were withdrawing across the Rappahannock—beaten yet again.

A year earlier the Confederacy had faced what seemed certain disaster, but Lee and his brave soldiers had rescued the southern cause. Ahead lay a summer in which to win or lose the war.

FOUR

TIDES IN THEIR TURNINGS

★

ROBERT E. LEE looked north in the late spring of 1863. Under his command, the Army of Northern Virginia had won astounding victories; yet he was worried. Even victories cost the South men and supplies it could not replace. The army had lost thirteen thousand soldiers at Chancellorsville, including Stonewall Jackson, mortally wounded by a nervous Confederate sentry. The battle had cost the North nearly seventeen thousand, but the Union seemed to have endless reserves. Every time Lee whipped the Army of the Potomac, it came back stronger than ever.

Meanwhile, the Confederacy was in deep trouble in the west. A Confederate attempt to reclaim lost ground late in 1862 had ended in bloody Union victories at Perryville, Kentucky, and Stones River, Tennessee. Now a large Union army under General William S. Rosecrans was preparing to march on Chattanooga, Tennessee, to force the Confederates out of the state.

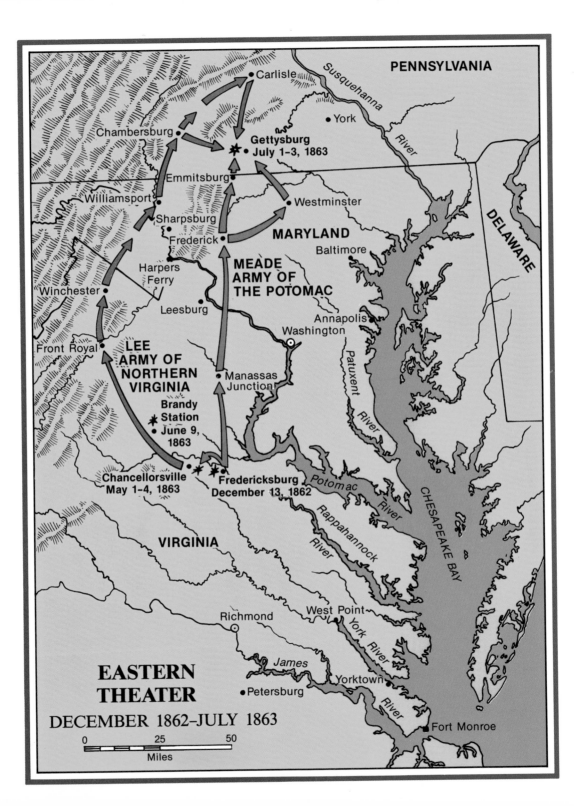

PENNSYLVANIA

Susquehanna River

Carlisle

York

Chambersburg

Gettysburg
July 1-3, 1863

Emmitsburg

Williamsport

Sharpsburg

Westminster

Frederick

MARYLAND

Harpers
Ferry

Baltimore

MEADE
ARMY OF
THE POTOMAC

Winchester

Leesburg

Front Royal

Annapolis

Washington

LEE
ARMY OF
NORTHERN
VIRGINIA

Manassas
Junction

Patuxent River

Brandy
Station
June 9,
1863

CHESAPEAKE BAY

Chancellorsville
May 1-4, 1863

Fredericksburg
December 13, 1862

Potomac River

Rappahannock River

VIRGINIA

York River

Richmond

West Point

James

Yorktown

**EASTERN
THEATER**

DECEMBER 1862–JULY 1863

Petersburg

Fort Monroe

0   25   50

Miles

DELAWARE

Farther west, General Grant was on the move again, pushing south along the Mississippi to split the Confederacy in two. One great obstacle remained for Grant's Union army — the city of Vicksburg, Mississippi. Protected by a steep bluff facing the river, scores of cannons, and twenty thousand Confederate soldiers, Vicksburg defied all attackers. But Lee knew that Grant was a very determined general.

Grant's army camped on the west side of the Mississippi across from Vicksburg in April 1863. Grant studied the city. Only a fool would send men charging up that steep bluff into the teeth of the city's defenses. He would have to move downstream, cross the river, and attack Vicksburg from the rear. Grant's men worked their way south through the swamps, fighting rain, mud, insects, snakes, and fever. The Union gunboat fleet ran past the blazing cannons of Vicksburg on the dark night of April 16. With army and navy united below the city, Grant ordered his men across to the east side of the river. For the next month, they fought to cut off Vicksburg, while its defenders battled to keep the roads and railroad open. Finally, the Confederates retreated within the walls of Vicksburg. Grant's army settled down to starve the city into surrender.

Far away in Virginia, Lee knew that he must do something to turn the tide of war running against the Confederacy in the West. If he could crush the Army of the Potomac once and for all, Grant and Rosecrans would have to rush troops east, leaving Vicksburg and Chattanooga in Confederate hands. With luck, Great Britain and France would at last throw their weight behind the Confederacy. Most important, a great victory might so dispirit the North that its people would force Lincoln to ask for peace.

Lee was still outnumbered, but he had great confidence in his tough veterans. He would take them north to threaten Washington, Baltimore, and Philadelphia. On the march through Maryland and Pennsylvania, they would gather badly needed supplies. General Hooker's Army of the Potomac would chase Lee's Army of Northern Virginia. And, when the time was right, Lee would turn and crush the Union army.

On June 4, 1863, Lee set his army on the road north. It took several days for the Army of the Potomac to take up the chase. For three weeks, the two armies marched north. On June 28, the Union soldiers heard that they had a new commander. Tired of Hooker's constant complaining, Lincoln had replaced him with General George Gordon Meade, a tough, crusty engineer called "Old Snapping Turtle" by his men. Meade pushed his army hard, determined to find Lee.

The greatest battle in American history began almost by chance near the small town of Gettysburg, Pennsylvania, on July 1, 1863. Confederate infantry searching for shoes ran into Union cavalry. Generals near the scene rushed in more troops. Before Lee and Meade knew it, they had a major battle on their hands.

The first day of the Battle of Gettysburg went the Confederates' way, as they pushed the Union troops through the town and up a ridge topped with a cemetery. That night Meade brought more troops to Cemetery Ridge and established a strong line bristling with cannons. The next day, Lee launched powerful attacks to break the left and right ends of the Union line. In fierce fighting, Meade's men threw back the Confederates. On the third day, Lee hit the center of the Union line with a great charge led by General George Pickett. It was a terrible mistake; Union cannon and rifle fire cut down Lee's men by the thousands.

The Battle of Gettysburg cost Lee a third of his army. Instead of winning a great victory, the Army of Northern Virginia had suffered a great defeat. On the night of July 4, it began the long retreat home. That same day, the starving defenders of Vicksburg surrendered to General Grant.

The tide of war had turned against the South for good, but the Confederacy fought on. President Davis and General Lee still hoped that the rising cost of the war would so sicken the North that Lincoln would lose the presidential election of 1864. Perhaps a new president would make peace and let the South leave the Union. But Lincoln had at last found fighting generals to lead the battle-hardened soldiers of the North. The largest and best-equipped armies in the nation's history prepared to crush the Confederacy.

Marching southeast from Murfreesboro, Tennessee, General Rosecrans's army forced the Confederates out of

Above: On July 3, 1863, General Robert E. Lee hurled Pickett's Charge against the center of the Union line at Gettysburg. The "high tide of the Confederacy" broke just short of victory in one of the great turning points of the war.

Left: The ferocious fighting at Gettysburg left Union and Confederate dead strewn across the battlefield. Of some 163,000 soldiers engaged, more than 51,000 were killed, wounded, or captured in the costliest battle in the history of North America.

Chattanooga. The Confederates struck back south of the city at Chickamauga Creek, Georgia, on September 19, 1863. Union General George H. Thomas, "the Rock of Chickamauga," saved the Union army in a hard-fought defense before retreating to the city. Grant—now commander of all the western armies—arrived to find Rosecrans's army bottled up in Chattanooga. He fired Rosecrans and took personal control. At the Battle of Missionary Ridge in late November, the Union troops broke out of Chattanooga and sent the Confederate army tumbling into Georgia. Grant reorganized his army and set it marching toward Atlanta in two large wings under Generals Thomas and William T. Sherman.

In March 1864, Lincoln called Grant to Washington to take command of all the Union armies. The one-time failure became the first three-star general in the United States Army since George Washington. Grant gave his orders. Sherman, now commanding the western armies, was to march through Georgia, destroying everything in his way. Meanwhile, Grant would take personal charge of the Army of the Potomac with Meade as his deputy. The time had come to fight Bobby Lee to the finish.

The Army of the Potomac crossed the Rapidan River west of Fredericksburg, Virginia, on May 4. Near the scene of so many other desperate battles, the armies of North and South met in a rough land of forest, brush, and swamp called the Wilderness. Day after day, they slugged it out.

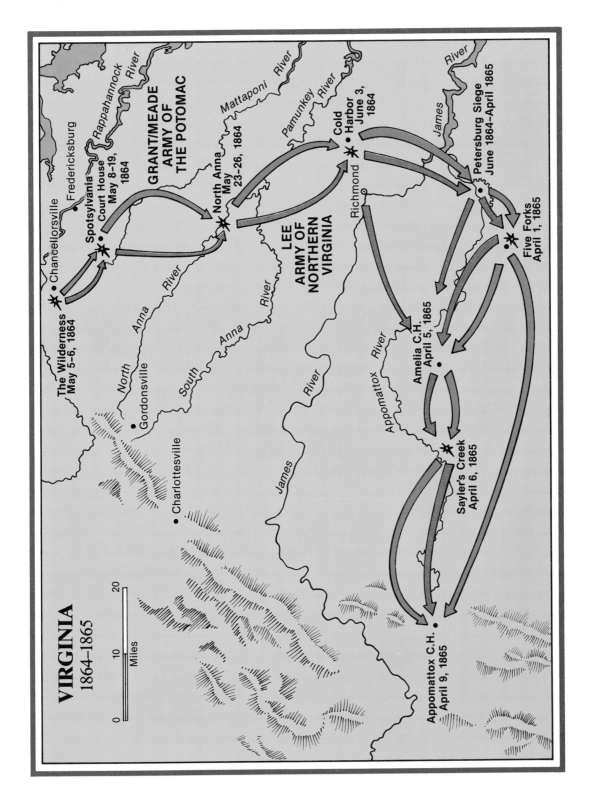

VIRGINIA
1864-1865

20

10

0

Miles

Chancellorsville

Fredericksburg

Spotsylvania
Court House
May 8-19,
1864

The Wilderness
May 5-6, 1864

GRANT/MEADE
ARMY OF
THE
POTOMAC

Rappahannock
River

Mattaponi
River

Pamunkey River

North Anna
May
23-26, 1864

North
Anna
River

South
Anna
River

Gordonsville

Charlottesville

LEE
ARMY OF
NORTHERN
VIRGINIA

James
River

Appomattox
River

Richmond

Cold
Harbor
June 3,
1864

River

James
River

Petersburg Siege
June 1864–April 1865

Five Forks
April 1, 1865

Amelia C.H.
April 5, 1865

Sayler's Creek
April 6, 1865

Appomattox C.H.
April 9, 1865

Unable to break through toward Richmond, Grant moved southeast. At the crossroads of Spotsylvania, there was another terrific fight. Lee's line held, and again Grant moved southeast. He was losing two soldiers for every one of Lee's, but he could replace his losses. This time the Army of the Potomac was not going to retreat.

The crafty Lee used every trick he knew, but the Army of the Potomac kept pushing. At Cold Harbor, Virginia, in early June, the Union army again tried to break through toward Richmond, only to suffer more frightful losses. Grant again moved southeast, crossing the James River and forcing his way to Petersburg, Virginia. From June 17 to June 22, Grant tried to break the Confederate line at Petersburg. The attacks failed, and after five weeks of the heaviest fighting of the war, the two armies finally rested. Lee had stopped Grant short of Richmond, but unlike McClellan and so many other Union generals, Grant did not run away. His army settled in to shell and starve the Confederate defenders into defeat.

William Tecumseh Sherman, the commander of the Union's other great army, had no plans to give up either. Sherman's men battered their way to Atlanta. Hopelessly outnumbered, the Confederates fought battle after battle. Finally on September 2, Lincoln received a telegram from Sherman: "Atlanta is ours, and fairly won."

The capture of Atlanta gave Lincoln's popularity a huge boost. On November 8, 1864, he was reelected, soundly de-

Right: Lincoln had found fighting commanders at last. Left to right they are: Admirals David D. Porter and David G. Farragut, Generals William T. Sherman, George H. Thomas, Ulysses S. Grant, and Philip H. Sheridan.

Below: In the spring of 1864, General Ulysses S. Grant marched south into the Wilderness at the beginning of the war's greatest campaign. Although defeated in the desperate Battle of Spotsylvania (shown here), Grant kept moving, determined to overwhelm Lee with numbers.

feating "Little Mac" McClellan, the Democratic candidate. The South's last hope for independence faded. Still it would not surrender. Confederate General John Bell Hood made a dash for Nashville, Tennessee, in a desperate attempt to cut Sherman's supply line. General Thomas got there first and destroyed Hood's army in the Battle of Nashville on December 15, 1864.

Residents of Atlanta, Georgia, prepare to flee as General William T. Sherman's huge Union army closes in on the city. "War is hell," Sherman said, and proved it by cutting a path of destruction across Georgia and the Carolinas.

The price of terrible responsibility is etched in
the faces of the two greatest generals of the war: Robert E. Lee and
Ulysses S. Grant. Unable to hold out against Grant's overwhelming
numbers, Lee surrendered near Appomattox Court House,
Virginia, on April 9, 1865.

Beyond Atlanta lay the rich farmlands of Georgia. Sherman set out to destroy the war-making abilities of the region. The Union army's "march to the sea" left a trail of destruction nearly 300 miles (500 km) long and often 60 miles (100 km) wide. On December 20, Sherman captured Savannah, Georgia, and turned north to bring total war to the Carolinas.

At Petersburg, Virginia, soldiers of North and South were learning the horrors of siege warfare. Grant's men pushed their trenches toward the city, fighting their way forward yard by yard. Lee's men threw back attack after bloody attack. Finally, the pressure was too much. On April 2, 1865, after more than nine months of fighting around Petersburg, Lee's line broke.

A week later, it was over. President Davis and his government fled Richmond. Grant's mighty army chased Lee's starving few. Trapped near Appomattox Court House, Virginia, Lee gave up the fight: "There is nothing left for me to do but go and see General Grant."

The two generals met at a small farmhouse on the afternoon of April 9, 1865. Lee — tall, erect, and dignified in his splendid uniform — arrived first on his beautiful gray horse. Grant rode up a few minutes later, his trousers and boots spattered with mud and only the general's stars on the shoulders of his private's uniform showing his rank.

Lee and Grant shook hands and talked for a few minutes about the old days when they had served in the army of an undivided nation. Grant offered generous surrender terms: The Confederate soldiers could go home on the promise not to fight again. They would be given food and allowed to keep their horses and mules. Most important, the United States government would not punish them for the years they had fought against the Union.

Pleased by Grant's generosity, Lee agreed, and the generals parted. When Union cannons started firing to celebrate the surrender, Grant ordered them stopped. His army should not celebrate the defeat of the brave soldiers of the South. "The war is over," he said, "The rebels are our countrymen again."

FIVE

WITH MALICE TOWARD NONE

★

WHILE the fighting still raged near Appomattox Court House, a tall, gaunt man in black walked the streets of Richmond. For four long years, Abraham Lincoln had guided the nation through the worst nightmare in its history. Now the end was nearing, and Lincoln wanted to see the capital city of those who had tried to divide the Union. A huge crowd of black people gathered around him, crying and singing, "Glory to God. Hallelujah." Some shyly touched the man they called "Father Abraham." One former slave threw himself on his knees before the president. Deeply moved, Lincoln reached out to him: "Don't kneel to me. . . . Kneel to God only, and thank Him for the liberty you enjoy hereafter."

Two weeks later, Abraham Lincoln's body lay in state beneath the high dome of the nation's Capitol. On the evening of Good Friday, April 14, 1865, the actor John Wilkes Booth,

The actor John Wilkes Booth, a Southern sympathizer, shot
President Lincoln during a play at Ford's Theater in Washington,
on the evening of April 14, 1865. Lincoln died early the next morning.

an embittered Southern sympathizer, had fired a single bullet into Lincoln's head while the president sat watching a stage play at Ford's Theater in Washington. Lincoln joined the hundreds of thousands who had shed their blood in the American Civil War.

The healing of the nation's wounds took many years. Lee, Grant, and many other veterans of the great battles tried to bring North and South together in friendship, but bitterness over the war would trouble the nation for decades. For black people the road would be particularly hard as they struggled for full political and social equality.

Yet all the suffering was not in vain. Northerners and Southerners alike dedicated themselves to rebuilding the nation. Restored, the Union became stronger than ever. The thousands of factories constructed to produce the supplies of war turned to making the goods of peace. Great cities blossomed. Settlement expanded westward, filling up the

Freed from slavery, black Americans set out on the long road to equality as the nation began the difficult task of healing the wounds of the Civil War.

wilderness and adding new states to the Union. A generation after the war, a strong and unified United States would be the equal of any nation on earth.

As Lincoln knew, power brings responsibilities for nations as well as individuals. More than a century after the Civil War, Lincoln's words to a war-torn nation still speak to the heart of our responsibility as citizens of a Union ever in the making:

With malice toward none, with charity for all, with firmness in the right as God gives us to see the right, let us strive on to finish the work we are in, to bind up the nation's wounds, to care for him who shall have borne the battle, . . . [and] to do all which may achieve and cherish a just and lasting peace among ourselves and with all nations.

(Second Inaugural Address, March 5, 1865)

APPENDIX A
LEADERS OF THE CIVIL WAR

UNION

President Abraham Lincoln
(1809–65)

Former President James Buchanan
(1791–1868)

Senator Stephen A. Douglas
(1813–61)

Lt. Gen. Ulysses S. Grant
(1822–85)

Maj. Gen. Don Carlos Buell
(1818–98)

Maj. Gen. Ambrose E. Burnside
(1824–81)

Maj. Gen. Henry W. Halleck
(1815–72)

Maj. Gen. Joseph Hooker
(1814–79)

Maj. Gen. George B. McClellan
(1826–85)

Maj. Gen. Irvin McDowell
(1818–85)

Maj. Gen. George G. Meade
(1815–72)

Maj. Gen. John Pope
(1822–92)

Maj. Gen. William S. Rosecrans
(1819–98)

Maj. Gen. William T. Sherman
(1820–91)

Maj. Gen. George H. Thomas
(1816–70)

Admiral David G. Farragut
(1801–70)

CONFEDERATE

President Jefferson Davis
(1808–89)

Gen. Robert E. Lee
(1807–70)

Gen. Pierre G. T. Beauregard
(1818–93)

Gen. Braxton Bragg
(1817–76)*

Gen. John Bell Hood
(1831–79)

Gen. Albert Sidney Johnston
(1803–62)

Gen. Joseph E. Johnston
(1807–91)

Lt. Gen. Thomas J. "Stonewall" Jackson
(1824–63)

Lt. Gen. John C. Pemberton
(1814–81)*

—————————

*Officers not mentioned in text.

APPENDIX B
MAJOR BATTLES OF THE CIVIL WAR

NAME*	DATE	LOCATION
First Bull Run (First Manassas)	July 21, 1861	Manassas Junction, Virginia
Shiloh (Pittsburg Landing)	April 6–7, 1862	Pittsburg Landing, Tennessee
New Orleans	April 24–25, 1862	New Orleans, Louisiana
Fair Oaks (Seven Pines)	May 31, 1862	Outside Richmond, Virginia
Shenandoah Valley	March–June, 1862	Shenandoah Valley, Virginia
The Seven Days	June 26–July 1, 1862	Outside Richmond, Virginia
Second Bull Run (Second Manassas)	August 29–30, 1862	Manassas Junction, Virginia
Antietam (Sharpsburg)	September 17, 1862	Sharpsburg, Maryland
Perryville	October 8, 1862	Perryville, Kentucky
Fredericksburg	December 13, 1862	Fredericksburg, Virginia
Stones River (Murfreesboro)	December 31, 1862–January 2, 1863	Murfreesboro, Tennessee
Chancellorsville	May 1–4, 1863	Chancellorsville, Virginia
Gettysburg	July 1–3, 1863	Gettysburg, Pennsylvania
Vicksburg	April–July, 1863	Vicksburg, Mississippi
Chickamauga	September 19–20, 1863	Chickamauga Creek, Georgia
Missionary Ridge	November 23–25, 1863	Chattanooga, Tennessee
The Wilderness and Spotsylvania	May 4–20, 1864	Vicinity of Fredericksburg, Virgina
Cold Harbor	June 3, 1864	Cold Harbor, Virginia
Atlanta	July 18–September 1, 1864	Atlanta, Georgia
Nashville	December 15, 1864	Nashville, Tennessee
Petersburg	June 15, 1864–April 2, 1865	Petersburg, Virginia

*For those battles that had different names in North and South, the Southern name is in parentheses.

COMMANDER		
UNION	**CONFEDERATE**	**OUTCOME**
Irvin McDowell	Joseph E. Johnston	Union army's first advance against the Confederacy ends in a disaster
Ulysses S. Grant	Albert S. Johnston	Confederates fail to halt Union effort to split the South along the Mississippi River
David G. Farragut	Various	Union navy captures Confederacy's largest city
George B. McClellan	Joseph E. Johnston	Confederates halt Union army's advance on Richmond
Various	Thomas J. Jackson	Jackson defeats small Union armies and blocks reinforcements for Union army attacking Richmond
George B. McClellan	Robert E. Lee	Lee's Army of Northern Virginia drives back Union attempt to capture Richmond
John Pope	Robert E. Lee	Lee and Jackson soundly defeat a Union Army
George B. McClellan	Robert E. Lee	McClellan turns back Lee's first invasion of the North, but misses the chance to deliver a crushing blow
Don Carlos Buell	Braxton Bragg	Confederate invasion of Kentucky turned back
Ambrose E. Burnside	Robert E. Lee	Union attempt to advance on Richmond ends in disaster
William S. Rosecrans	Braxton Bragg	Confederate invasion of Tennessee defeated
Joseph Hooker	Robert E. Lee	Lee brilliantly defeats yet another Union attempt to advance on Richmond
George G. Meade	Robert E. Lee	Lee's second invasion of the North ends in defeat in the war's greatest battle
Ulysses S. Grant	John C. Pemberton	Fall of Vicksburg on July 4 wins Union control of the Mississippi
William S. Rosecrans	Braxton Bragg	Confederate victory briefly halts Union invasion of Georgia
Ulysses S. Grant	Braxton Bragg	Union victory sends Confederates retreating into Georgia
Ulysses S. Grant	Robert E. Lee	Unable to break through toward Richmond, Grant moves southeast
Ulysses S. Grant	Robert E. Lee	Union attempt to break the Confederate line costs 8,000 casualties in eight minutes
William T. Sherman	John Bell Hood	Atlanta, the key city in the Deep South, falls to the Union army
George H. Thomas	John Bell Hood	Desperate Confederate attempt to regain the offensive ends in total defeat
Ulysses S. Grant	Robert E. Lee	After nine months of siege warfare, Union breakout leads to surrender of main Confederate army at Appomattox Court House on April 9, 1865

SUGGESTED READING

Carter, Alden R. *The Battle of Gettysburg.* New York: Franklin Watts, 1989.

Carter, Hodding. *Robert E. Lee and the Road of Honor.* New York: Random House, 1955.

Catton, Bruce. *The American Heritage Picture History of the Civil War.* New York: Doubleday, 1960.

Freedman, Russell. *Lincoln: A Photobiography.* New York: Clarion, 1987.

Goldston, Robert. *The Coming of the Civil War.* New York: Macmillan, 1972.

Jordan, Robert Paul. *The Civil War.* Washington, D.C.: National Geographic, 1969.

Kantor, MacKinlay. *Lee and Grant at Appomattox.* New York: Random House, 1950.

Weidhorn, Manfred. *Robert E. Lee.* New York: Atheneum, 1988.

Windrow, Martin. *The Civil War Rifleman.* New York: Franklin Watts, 1985.

INDEX

Page numbers in *italics* refer to illustrations.

ABOUT THE AUTHOR

ALDEN R. CARTER is a versatile writer for children and young adults. He has written nonfiction books on electronics, supercomputers, radio, Illinois, Shoshoni Indians, the American Revolution, the People's Republic of China, the Alamo, the Battle of Gettysburg, the Colonial Wars, the War of 1812, the Mexican War, and the Spanish-American War. His novels *Growing Season* (1984), *Wart, Son of Toad* (1985), *Sheila's Dying* (1987), and *Up Country* (1989) were named to the American Library Association's annual list, Best Books for Young Adults. His fifth novel, *RoboDad,* was honored as Best Children's Fiction Book of 1990 by the Society of Midland Authors. Mr. Carter lives with his wife, Carol, and their children, Brian Patrick and Siri Morgan, in Marshfield, Wisconsin.